Koala

Rod Theodorou

D0552021

700021439900

Heinemann
LIBRARY

H www.heinemann.co.uk
Visit our website to find out more information about **Heinemann Library** books.

To order:
☎ Phone 44 (0) 1865 888066
▤ Send a fax to 44 (0) 1865 314091
▢ Visit the Heinemann Bookshop at www.heinemann.co.uk to browse our catalogue and order online.

First published in Great Britain by Heinemann Library, Halley Court, Jordan Hill, Oxford OX2 8EJ, a division of Reed Educational and Professional Publishing Ltd.
Heinemann is a registered trademark of Reed Educational & Professional Publishing Limited.

OXFORD MELBOURNE AUCKLAND JOHANNESBURG BLANTYRE
GABORONE IBADAN PORTSMOUTH NH (USA) CHICAGO

Designed by Ron Kamen
Illustrations by Dewi Morris/Robert Sydenham
Originated by Ambassador Litho Ltd.
Printed in Hong Kong/China

ISBN 0431 00136 7 (hardback)   ISBN 0431 00153 7 (paperback)
06 05 04 03 02 01   06 05 04 03 02
10 9 8 7 6 5 4 3 2 1   10 9 8 7 6 5 4 3 2 1

British Library Cataloguing in Publication Data
Theodorou, Rod
    Koala. - (Animals in Danger)
    1.Koala - Juvenile literature 2.Endangered species - Juvenile literature
    I.Title
    599.2'5

Acknowledgements
The Publishers would like to thank the following for permission to reproduce photographs: Ardea: pp8, 12, Jean-Paul Ferrero pp17, 25, Francois Gohier p4, Martin W Grosnick p4; Bat Conservation International: Merlin D Tuttle p4; BBC: John Cancalosi pp6, 9, 19, Georgette Douwma p13, Tim Edward p18, Steven David Miller p20; Bruce Coleman: David Austen p27, John Cancalosi p16, John Shaw p21; Mary Evans Picture Library: p22; FLPA: Terry Whittaker p24; Natural Science Photos: p7; NHPA: p15, Martin Harvey p14; Oxford Scientific Films: pp5, 11; State Library of Queensland, Australia: p23; John Waterhouse: p26.

Cover photograph reproduced with permission of Still Pictures.

Our thanks to Henning Dräger at WWF-UK for his comments in the preparation of this book.

Every effort has been made to contact copyright holders of any material reproduced in this book. Any omissions will be rectified in subsequent printings if notice is given to the Publisher.

Contents

Any words appearing in the text in bold, **like this**, are explained in the Glossary.

Animals in danger

polar bear

grey bat

cheetah

All over the world, more than 25,000 animal **species** are in danger. Some are in danger because their home is being **destroyed**. Many are in danger because people hunt them.

This book is about koalas and why they are in danger. Unless people learn to look after them, koalas will become **extinct**. We will only be able to find out about them from books like this.

What are koalas?

Koalas are **mammals**. Many people think koalas are like bears, but they are really closer to kangaroos because they are **marsupials**.

Koalas like to live on their own. They usually come out at night. The koala is one of the national symbols of Australia.

What do koalas look like?

Koalas are medium-sized. They are coloured grey-brown with white patches. Their fur **protects** them from hot and cold weather and from rain. They have a round face and ears and a **snub** nose.

Koalas have sharp pointed claws and rough pads on their paws to help them climb trees. Their arms are almost the same length as their legs, which helps them to climb.

Where do koalas live?

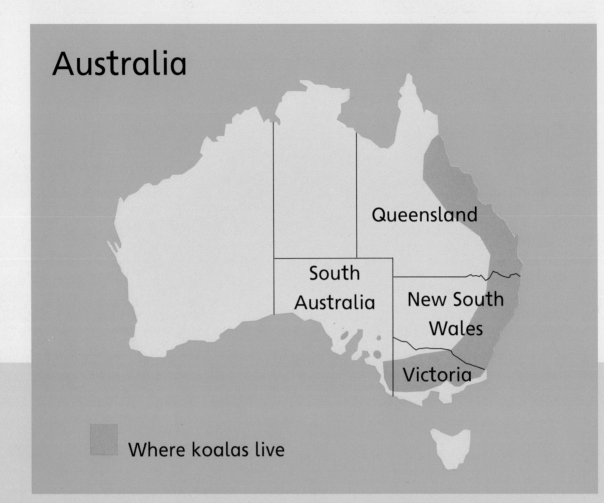

Australia

Queensland

South
Australia

New South
Wales

Victoria

Where koalas live

Koalas live in Australia. Most of them live in
Queensland, but there are also koalas in New
South Wales, Victoria and South Australia.

Koalas live in places where there are plenty of trees (usually **eucalyptus**). They mark their own trees with smells and scratches, so other koalas don't go near them.

What do koalas eat?

Koalas eat the oily leaves of **eucalyptus** trees. They have special teeth to help them eat the leaves. Koalas sometimes eat leaves from other trees, such as wattle, tea tree or paperbark.

Eucalyptus leaves are not very **nutritious** so koalas sleep for up to 20 hours a day to save **energy**. They eat at night, when it is cooler, to use up less energy and water.

Koala babies

Koalas **mate** between September and March. The babies are born 32 to 35 days later. **Female** koalas usually have one baby, every one or two years. The babies are called **joeys**.

When they are born, the babies are small, pink and hairless. They travel to their mother's **pouch**, where they climb in to feed on her milk and grow.

Looking after the babies

When they are about six months old, the **joeys** start peeping out of the **pouch**. They climb on to their mother's back and stay there for the next six months.

Koalas leave their mother and find their own home when they are about one year old. If the mother has no more babies, they stay with her for longer.

Unusual koala facts

Koalas speak to each other with grunts and soft clicking, squeaking and humming sounds. When koalas are very scared they make a loud cry like a baby screaming.

After coming out of their mother's **pouch**, koalas don't drink again! They get all their water from the leaves they eat. Koala means 'no drink' in the **Aboriginal** language.

How many koalas are there?

Australia is a huge country. At one time there were plenty of trees to feed hungry koalas. About 80 years ago there were millions of koalas living all over Australia.

Today the millions have disappeared. The Australian Koala Foundation believes that there are less than 65,000 koalas left.

Why is the koala in danger?

About 100 years ago, many people moved to Australia from other parts of the world. They brought diseases with them. Koalas catch diseases easily and many of them died.

Millions of koalas were shot for their furs. This trailer is full of them. By the 1930s koalas were nearly **extinct**. Because of this, there are very few koalas left today.

Why is the koala in danger?

Koalas need trees to live in and find food. Many trees have been cut down to make space for towns, roads and farms. This leaves nothing for the koalas to eat.

As towns are built near where koalas live, they are also hit by cars as they try to cross busy roads. Cats and dogs sometimes kill koalas.

How is the koala being helped?

Conservation groups are working to **protect** koalas, and the trees they need to survive. Special **reserves** have been built for koalas to live in.

Ill or hurt koalas, or koalas that have lost their mothers, are looked after at special koala hospitals. When the koalas are better, they are released back into the wild.

Koala factfile

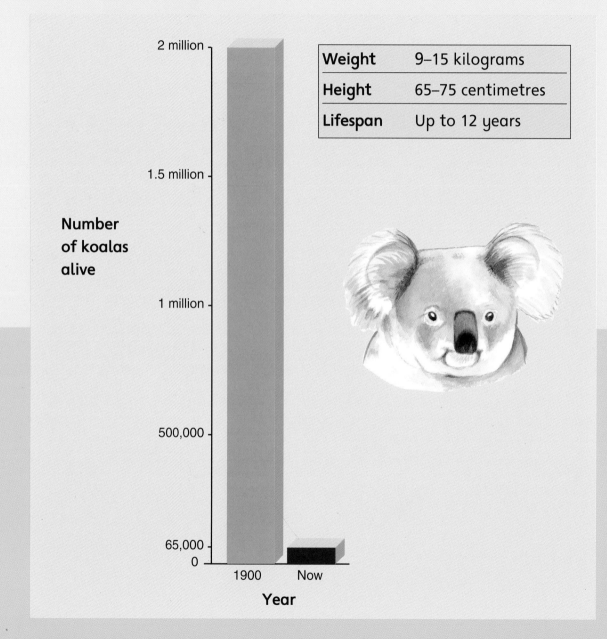

Weight	9–15 kilograms
Height	65–75 centimetres
Lifespan	Up to 12 years

Number of koalas alive

2 million
1.5 million
1 million
500,000
65,000
0

1900   Now

Year

World danger table

	Number that may have been alive 100 years ago	Number that may be alive today
Cheetah	135,000	15,000
Grey bat	6.3 million	900,000
Leatherback turtle	1 million females	39,000 females
Polar bear	710,000	24,000
Whooping crane	2100	400

There are thousands of other animals in the world that are in danger of becoming **extinct**. This table shows some of these animals.

Can you find out more about them?

Further reading, addresses and websites

Books

High in the Tree, Neecy Twinem, Charlesbridge Publishing Inc, 1998

Koalas, Nature Watch series, Denise Burt, Carolrhoda Books, 1997

Koalas, New True Book, Emilie Lepthien, Children's Press Inc, 1998

Koalas for Kids, Wildlife for Kids series, Kathy Feeney and John F. McGee, Creative Publishing International, 1996

The Koala is not a Bear!, Hannelore Sotzek and Bobbie Kalman, Crabtree Publishing Company, 1998

Organizations

Australian Koala Foundation:
1/40 Charlotte Street, Brisbane, QLD 4000, Australia ☎ 07 3229 7233

Friends of the Earth: UK - 26–28 Underwood Street, London N1 7JQ ☎ (020) 7490 1555
Australia - 312 Smith Street, Collingwood, VIC 3065 ☎ 03 9419 8700

Greenpeace: UK - Canonbury Villas, London N1 2PN ☎ (020) 7865 8100
Australia - Level 4, 39 Liverpool Street, Sydney, NSW 2000 ☎ 02 9261 4666

WWF: UK - Panda House, Weyside Park, Catteshall Lane, Godalming, Surrey GU7 1XR ☎ (01483) 426444
Australia - Level 5, 725 George Street Sydney, NSW 2000 ☎ 02 9281 5515

Useful websites

www.bbc.co.uk/nature
The BBC's animals site. Go to Really Wild for information on all sorts of animals, including fun activities, the latest news and links to programmes.

www.koala.net
The website of the Lone Pine Koala Sanctuary.

www.sandiegozoo.org
The world famous American San Diego Zoo's site.

www.savethekoala.com
The website of the Australian Koala Foundation.

www.wwf.org
WWF (World Wide Fund for Nature) is the world's largest independent conservation organization. WWF conserves wildlife and the natural environment for present and future generations.

Glossary

Aboriginal	people who first lived in Australia
conservation	looking after things, especially if they are in danger
destroyed	spoilt, broken or torn apart so it can't be used
energy	the power to move about and do things
eucalyptus	type of Australian tree with green leaves
extinct	dead and can never live again
female	girl or woman
joey	baby koala
mammal	animal with hair like a human or a dog. Mammals drink their mother's milk as a baby.
marsupial	kind of mammal that has a pouch
mate	when a male and a female come together to have babies
nutritious	food which is healthy and good for you
pouch	type of pocket on some animals' stomachs
protect	to look after. Some animals are protected by law.
reserve	place where animals are looked after
snub	small and flat
species	a group of the same animals or plants

Index